LAPS

LAPS

A Poem by
Michael Blumenthal

The University of Massachusetts Press
Amherst, 1984

Copyright © 1984 by

Michael Blumenthal

All rights reserved

Printed in the United States of America

Library of Congress Cataloging in Publication Data

Blumenthal, Michael.

Laps.

I. Title.

PS3552.L849L3   1984   813'.54   84–8601

ISBN 0–87023–459–5

ISBN 0–87023–460–9 (pbk.)

Laps has been published with the support of the

Literature Program of the National Endowment

for the Arts, a federal agency to which acknowledgment

is gratefully made.

Acknowledgments

The author wishes to gratefully acknowledge the support of the D.C. Commission on the Arts and Humanities and the Rockefeller Foundation, and most particularly the kind and generous staff of The Rockefeller Conference and Study Center (Villa Serbelloni) in Bellagio, Italy, among whose conducive and gentle confines the final sections of this poem were written and revised. Also thanks to the Corporation of Yaddo for a residency during which the final arrangement of the poems in their present sequence was completed.

Section 1 of this poem, in somewhat earlier form, appeared under the title "Going Deep" in the Spring 1983 issue of the *Kansas Quarterly*.

For those I have hurt,
in repentance.
For those who have hurt me,
in forgiveness.

I found some water, moving without a ripple,
Without a sound, clear to the very bottom,
You would not even think the water was even moving,
You could count the pebbles, and the silver willows
And poplars shaded the sloping banks. I stood there
Paused, dipped my toes in, waded to my knees,
And this was not enough. I took my clothes off
And hung them on a willow, bending over,
And plunged in naked, and while I beat the waters
With one stroke and another, and turned and glided,
I thought I heard a curious kind of murmur
From deep down under . . . wherever I moved,
There seemed to be a pool, and even quicker
Than I can tell the story I was changed
To a stream of water.

OVID, *Metamorphoses*
TRANSLATED BY ROLFE HUMPHRIES

Now I will you to be a bold swimmer . . .
WHITMAN, *Song of Myself*

"How strange men are," she said, because
she could not think of anything else to say.
"They spend their lives fighting against priests,
and then give prayerbooks as gifts."

GABRIEL GARCIA MARQUEZ,
One Hundred Years of Solitude

LAPS

Prologue

Oh Patron Aristippus of the flesh,
who thought of pleasure as the final
 source,
who watched the soul contort, the body
 thrash,
but held to his resolve without remorse,
Oh sweet, immoral bard who didn't see
the soul's lot cast with dull Divinity,
who didn't hesitate to praise, to name
encyclicals of lust and greed and shame.
Oh sacred Father of desire,
who found duty good, but pleasure
 higher,
might I, a moral Jew, be blessed
to find the key to life here, half undressed?
Might I call Moses fool, who split the sea,
while Pharoah lay with one, or two, or
 three?
I pray, dear philosophe of ethics in the
 moan
that I might come to wisdom here, alone
and swim with tear-starved gusto as I
 glide
from pleasure to pleasure, side to side.

Aristippus (ca. 435–360 B.C.) was the Greek philoso-
pher of Cyrene who founded the Cyrenaic school of
philosophy whose chief tenet was the primacy of pleasure
as a source of moral good. For the Cyrenaics, virtue was
seen as identical with the ability to enjoy sensuous and
other delights, and the scant philosophical fragments left
by Aristippus thus constitute the first coherent exposition
of the philosophy of hedonism.

Tired of everything I know,
I turn to what I do not know,
hoping to find where I am, hoping
to find where I know I must go.

The water sings in my ears.
In Singapore, wild girls whistle on the
    beach.
Birds nest in the grass, and I know
it is never too late to turn, never
too late to go where I must go.

Softly, softly, to turn softly,
to shake what must be shaken loose
and not break anything at all. To pry
the petals from the rose and not break
the flower; to treasure the moment
and not destroy the hour.

What does it mean to be in pain?
No more than that the rain is rain,
and flood flood. Deep we are, and deep
is where we have to go. As seed goes deep.
As rain goes deep to bring forth the
    flower.

As the worm must go deep to take us
    dustward.

The body
wanting some small perfection
and therefore
repeating itself.
And the beginning
of all repetition
seems original,
seems unrepeatable
and particular.
So here I am,
quick-kicked and stroking
across the pool,
my eyes like those
of some peculiar toad
in their plastic cups,
my fingers meeting
the cold concrete
for the first time,
sending the body
back under
with a deep breath
of pleasure
and inhalation,
transmitting
to the momentarily
quiet mind
the conflicting messages
of this strange harmony—
Arrival
        Beginning
                Repetition . . .

Order.

What a peculiar thing
the mind is,
what a strange legacy
of randomness and repetition,
a tiny teaapple
of hope and despondency
moving back and forth
over the lanes
of this life, the concrete
and imagined
boundaries, the saline
and chlorified air,
the bubbling surface
and the shrunk horizon.

And what a strange thing too
the body: an envelope
of flesh and necessity,
a loose coincidence
of orifice and appendage,
the soul's wet suit,
the mind's a cappella
accompaniment, the one note
so often out of tune
in the Vienna Boys' Choir
of the soul. It is
our time's sad icon,
its altar and its ark,
the prayer shawl
and epidermis
of our exploited longings.

So this, perhaps,
is a kind of prayer—
a litany
in which the body

reaches
for its own small portion
of heaven, in which
the self turns inward
to escape the self, so that
the sheer, unwavering dullness
might lead
to transcendence:
in these straight,
continuing lines, in the
swift, extended reach
of the arms
as the soul ripples out—
penumbral and
graceful, the body's
unwitting accomplice:
kept smoke
and shadow,
doused fire.

In the first three lanes,
beneath the water,
I see the "special children"
swimming, contending
against the chill
and the engulfing weight,
thrashing into the air
like wind-up dolls
as they rise over the deep,
as they stagger
against the sides.

One of them,
a boy, chalk-white
in his visage, his hands
held like paws
against his cheeks,
cries out
into the still air of the pool
like a loon
over Lake Nubinusit
or a sea gull
having a nightmare, eerie
and compelling. Another
bangs like a strayed duck
into the walls
and is retrieved
by his counselor.

They are "special" children,
I think to myself, only
in language. In fact,
they are merely us
with a slight accident,

a chromosomal lisp,
as in a beautiful boat
with a hole in its mainsail
or a young tulip
with a torn petal,
and in the sight of them
I see myself, I say: there
but for the grace of God
go I. And I go on.

What's perfecter than sleep
is waking bliss:
the body dreaming
in these quiet lanes,
the water tender as a kiss,
the bones so uncomplaining
as they arc and paddle
through the deep
and shallow of the pool.

Gleaming bodies
undulate and ooze
beneath my stare,
and on the streets,
against the glare
of light that tinsels
through the panes,
the passersby
now stop and stare,
their boozy breath reverberant
against the icy glass,
their feet at rest.

They all complain
about their bulging waists,
their dulling jobs,
expensive tastes.
They spend their sleep
in wishing they were slim
like those of us below,
awake, who swim.

6

Have you ever been to the zoo
and watched the sea lions?
What a nonterrestrial happiness!
What a small orgy of ecstasy
and rhapsodic movement,
as if to say: *This*
is happiness.

And in a better world
than this one,
I would nuzzle my nose
gently
between the legs
of the young girl beside me.
What an olfactory joy!
What a proboscitory gladness
I would feel! But this
is not California, this
is Washington, D.C.,
the nation's homely capital,
and happiness, like music,
is a private affair.

So I bury
my whiskers
back
into the sweet orifice
of my own thoughts:
a perfectly private sea lion,
a good citizen.

The sweet tintinnabulation
of water
in my ears
and thoughts of a skier
gliding, downhill,
over the packed
and glistening snow,
fluttering his long legs
as he shimmers through
the lanes, the wind whipping
like cold water into his face,
the shoulders churning like fins
through the net of the air,
this too is a kind of
swimming, a choreography
of bone and breath, of fine thoughts
reverberating through the whisked
and undulating brain
as it chaperons the body, as it
cruises, all but effortlessly,
through the ice-blue waters.

I think of those moments
of skiing past,
their complete presentness
and high pleasure
and of how, now, pleasure
requires a moral dimension,
something at least as lovely
and kind as a poem
to justify it. This, I
think to myself, approaching
the wall again, may be
one mark of manhood:
the turning outward of pleasure
toward something larger than itself,

this sense that burns
as I turn, that burns
to please you, who
are reading this, you
who turn too
as I swim on.

The young boy
swimming beside me,
some ersatz Tadzio
of the mind or spirit,
is he really
so beautiful? Or is it
only the air-brush
impressionism
of the water
that makes him so?

Turning my head
from within the bubbles
of my own exhalations,
I notice now
that almost all
of the bodies
are beautiful.
So maybe,
I think to myself,
letting my legs
for a moment
go limp, that's
what beauty is: a kind
of generalized forgetting
of small details,
a blur
that clarifies.

And so now,
traversing this pool
for the eighth time,
I find a new way
of saying
I love you:
I overlook.

9

No bones
about it, the body's
a beautiful thing,
so versatile in its
permutations, so capable,
like Keats' living hand.
Capable, that's
what I'd like to be:
capable of making something
as simply beautiful as
swimming is, a movement
at first difficult, almost
cumbersome, then
nearly automatic, and then
perfectly divine.

And so
the juxtaposition
of odd companions
leads frequently
to pleasure: this slight
and frequently random
intelligence, this aging
but still perfectly sound
body, those movements,
ecstatic, unpredictable,
in which I proceed
without purpose,
and those merely
expedient, in which
I turn only because
I must, giving form both
to the occasion and the poem,
as my lips, puckering
and unpuckering again
above the blue margin,
give form to the air.

After the rains left Macondo
in Garcia Marquez's *One
Hundred Years of Solitude*,
Aureliano Segundo asks the survivors
how they survived
the four years, eleven months
and two days of rain,
how they managed
to not go awash,
and all gave
the same answer: *swimming*.

Now here, a feeling
not unlike that of Verrocchio's *Baptism*
comes over me as I glide
through the water, my fingers
arced upward as in prayer,
my head bowed in a kind
of penance and forgetfulness.

So perhaps I too
will survive by swimming:
an amphibian moved first
by a stroke of genius, then
by a stroke of luck as I
weave through these waters,
a priest and a penitent
both at once, an expiator
of my own sins,
a quick eel, electric
in his own current.

A quiet calm
moves downward from the eyes,
the earth unraveling
into a veil of blue,
the body coddling forward
by its own small light.

A pulmonary happiness
invades the heart,
the phalanges adrumming
to the beat of flesh,
the timbered femur throbbing
in the painted lanes.

Slowly the beat
becomes an automatic song,
the body slicing forward
like a knife,
the breath sucked backward
through the bones,
the corpuscles
that bob and thresh.

And I continue
moving at this constant pace—
as if this were my only life,
as if my life were only flesh.

The transformation of stress
into inspiration
is what I'm after, I
now realize. And what
an inspiring thing it is
to be here, eating the meters
with my stride, thrusting
my warm face beneath the surface
like a large catfish, hardening
my own flesh toward bone
as I swallow these distances.
But too much thinking
can harden the heart, I
know it, unless thought's
just movement's shadow,
a small bird flying
in its heavy wake.

And why would a man
move this way
(the dull dittoing
of small increments,
the scrimped scissoring
of the legs) unless
some form of enlightenment
lay at the end of it?
And why get yourself
a large car, why jog
your mind into some
concrete graveyard, your
knees clicking like stones
against some outdoor icepath,
your teeth achatter? Just
remember how life began
to begin with: the first
amoeboids crawling like lice
from the murky waters,

the sweet increase
of the protozoa. *Just swim,*
I say to myself, *swim*
as if your life depended
on it: the expiatory waters
rippling to a swift wind,
the wind a breeze
of your own making.

The Angel Gabriel,
I woke from a dream
one night whispering,
is the imagination.
So now I imagine this
to be a far greater feat
than it really is,
a small Everest the body
can climb easily,
yet congratulate itself
on completing, the way
some consider abstinence
from chocolate or from
adultery a triumph
of the will.

Yet ambition
can be a terrible thing,
not for its ends, which
may be admirable, but
for its means,
which usually require
a gift for duplicity
and meanness, an error
of proportion.

But here
all's proportional:
the imagination is the dream
and the doing, an act
overcoming the desire
to stray from the act,
a complaint
embodying its own cure,
a movement
leading beyond itself

to a certain stillness
in which the elements
conjoin—
    Earth.
    Water.
    Air.
        My own small flame.

How Prussian of me,
I now realize,
to make of this act
of pure movement
and loss of thought
an act of thinking. Jung
would call me
a *thinking type*, which
implies that feeling
is my *inferior function*.

But Oh hell
what a feeling
of pleasure
these wet and baptismal
thoughts bring,
this turning of the head
sideways
and down, this
deepening rhythm
of the breath
as it mimics itself.

My eyes reopen now
in this concrete amnion,
noticing again
the smooth,
water-refined bodies
of the swimmers
beside me, savoring again
this rush of water
and flesh,

of hair,
and flying bone.

What is Jewish literature?
the scholars ask. Is a Jew,
say, swimming or a Jew
thinking about swimming
here, on the Sabbath, at
the Young Men's *Christian*
Association, still a Jew?
Or is he more like
Babel's horseman, merely
a rider with snipped genitals
and Angst? There are fellowships
to discuss such matters, I
remind myself, turning
my large and ethnic features
to the side for air, blowing
bubbles shaped like skullcaps
toward the wet. And if Moses
parted deep seas for my sires,
then why am I swimming now,
treading this blue pond for a
sign, combing the bottom
for a wisp of truth? What
golden calf do I worship
in this movement's name?
Whose homage do I take in vain
as I think these thoughts?

Thoughts like these,
so secular and wild despite
their seeming, are what
keep me moving as I ride
to pierce: an emigré afloat
in this wild diaspora, a seed
grown turgid with its own

movement, a survivor
in my own slow wake,
a *Shabbos goy*
who worships as he sins.

A misanthropic ardor
rises as I flip to find
a truant in my lane:
a *jeune* nymphotic *fille* in red
who uddles forward
toward my outstretched arms
and makes me think,
at first, of: *bed*.

But here, where rhythm
and repeat are all I've got,
I'm anti-amorous
and territorial to the core:
Darwinian, I lust for space
and space . . . and more.
So now I swerve, midway
across my light blue lane
and rise to shout: *You're
in my way! Get out!*

As if she'd heard
before I even spoke,
she coddles left
and disappears
before my blinking eyes
like smoke. I stroke again
to find her out of sight,
and am left single
in my lane again
and free to think: *Dear,
where will you be
tonight?*

Is life
a bitch? Can a man
tire of his own breathlessness
like an old hound, or is
a mere continuing enough
to revive him, wash
the film from his eyes
and urge him onward?

Questions like these
would not seem the subject
of swimming, but
they *are* its subject:
the deep innuendo of all
continuing, the mythology
of breath, the wisdom
of starting over.

And why else
would a man pause
midway
through his own ritual,
but to examine
its meaning, to ask himself
whether the time
might not be ripe
to change strokes,
begin again
in a different rhythm—
the legs tensed,
the arms stationary,
the eyes obsessively focused,
looking inward.

In the fallopian tubes
what a strange beginning
it must have been:
the ravenous swimmers,
long-legged, eager,
fluttering wildly
into the dark of the cervix,
along the lanes of the vagina,
and surfacing only to find
the stubborn concrete
of the ovum: unwelcoming,
impenetrable.

I have seen pictures of it,
magnified thousands of times
from the life of the sea urchin
and it reminds me,
now, of myself,
of what I might do
weren't I human, a person
whose urge to persist,
continue, repeat himself endlessly
is larger than any obstacle,
sillier, more meaningful.

Were I not such a man,
were I, say, merely
the small seed I began as,
I might stop here,
flutter my legs for a while
in ennui and frustration
and bang my soft head
against the intractable concrete.

Who knows
but that I might turn,
disgusted with my own silly ritual

and give up
on what I had set out
to accomplish. Who knows
but that I might just
turn back without breathing
and not surface again.
I might just die of my own trying:
a futile flapper
in a well of my own choosing,
a father to no one,
an alien in my own country.

Whether it is better
for the heart to beat
rapidly
in some aquatic proving ground
or simply
in a low hum, to attest
to the cerebral indolence
of some infinite sitting,
no one knows. Experts
disagree. Roethke,
as you may know, died
while swimming
near Puget Sound.

But we must
all die. So my heart
flutters and catapults
across the pool,
a seismograph
of its own eruptions.
What a vain hope
of continuum, what
a silly place, you
might say, to look
for divinity,
the kind of thing
only a Buddhist
with a Ford
Foundation fellowship
might do. But simply
as pleasure, as libretto
to the loss of the sonorous self,
what delight, what quietude:
not a single tree
turning to matchsticks
in my rippling wake.

What a strange and exotic animal
the aweto is: how it burrows
beneath the parched and lovely
earth of New Zealand,
singlemindedly ravenous
for the one seed which,
devoured, will expand,
germinate, fissure out
within its host's small body
until, large beyond the bounds
of what contains it, it sprouts
right through the aweto's stomach,
on through the mouth,
and continues through
the aweto's small brain,
exploding it.

And think too
of the limpet,
that tent-shaped mollusk
so ravenous to continue
that, when attacked, though
mortally wounded, it will
regenerate its own
innards, creating
from its small purgatory
a rebirth, a kind of
modest perpetuity,
a going on
beyond its own possibilities.

Now, some ten laps beyond
what I thought was fatigue
and thirsty
for what I know will
undo me, I feel a kinship
with both these animals:

the one yearning
for precisely what destroys it,
the other flowering out
beyond its limitations.

And diving now,
tight-lipped, from the surface
as I prepare to turn
for the twentieth time,
I think of these ironies
and of water, and of how
it too could fill us with
its own weight until we drown,
how each survives
by taming what he needs,
how movement rescues stillness
from its own dead weight
and, doing so, becomes
that stillness.

Quiet with these thoughts,
I rise once more
toward the surface,
smooth as a penguin,
wingless and exotic
in this damp continuing.

A terrible *Gemütlichkeit*
now overtakes the bones
as they move through
these waters, a kind
of indolence no doubt
resulting from the evenness
of movement, the parabolas
and sweet elegance
of Tintoretto's *Leda
and the Swan* as the arms
and torso endlessly
repeat themselves,
as they elongate out
into the water's canvas.

And still
it's an old story:
the seemingly frivolous
as a source of divinity—
the endless tedium
of the Japanese tea ceremony,
the slow progress
of the tzaddik
up the steep hill
to the synagogue,
the infinite cantata
of rain. All virtue,
then, I say to myself,
striking the cold concrete
for the twenty-first time,
is a kind of patience,
a willingness
to sweat it out,
to turn around,
to keep on.

The pleopods of the blue crab:
loving, gesticular, the instruments
of coitus and swimming, what
a lovely coupling of functions
they perform, what a strange symbiosis
of lust and movement. So, too,
these swimmerets of mine, having
just this morning circled my wife,
now surround the water,
pushing it, parting it, reshaping
it in swilled and circular motions,
jettisoning it sideways
and beneath me as I ride
the wetness, as I uddle and amble
and glide through the damp, coital
and drenched in my own thinking.

But love in the water
is not a smooth thing, for humans
at least: the difficult minglings
of love-oil and water, the perils
of panting beneath the surface,
the diminution of flavor. I
have tried it: in a small pool,
abandoned, fenced in, isolated
in some dark suburbia. She
was lovely, in water, like
a scintillant eel—sensuous
and serpentlike, tempting me
toward her.

I had pulled off
her bathing suit, peeling it
like Saran Wrap
from her orifices, tossing it
like some aquatic Don Juan
from the water, and nestled her

against the concrete. There,
in the shallow end, beneath the light
fluorescence of the summer moon,
I licked the small pearls of water
from her breasts, I thrust
my small scepter of horniness
back and forth inside her.

But now, I hold my body
true to its subject: I cup
my large hands like twin claws
beneath the water, I plunge
forward, stroking, dreaming
of my wife, and of all women,
embraced, whom I have
loved, and of where
they might be now, in some
new body of water, nestled,
surrounded, embraced
by other lovers, each
to his own wetness
and moving on.

Like a hydrofoil
flying over Lake Como
in late summer, sluicing
through the waters, raising
its metaled arms
between Bellagio and Tellagio,
I now cruise
the concrete outposts
of this natatory lake, feeling
the fine and robust weight
of my arms, stretching
my two hundred and eight bones
through the clarifying,
chlorifying wet. Now
eight strokes and harder
to the breath, I span
this distance purposefully quick,
the taste of some small pride
summoned to my lips, the thought
of unimpeded air and wine
resounding in my brain.

I pass the lovely swimmer
on my left, her nipples
puckered in an amber suit,
her buttocks churning
like twin moons
above the plashing swill.
And as I place my arms
again against the sides
and push my body, dripping,
through the air, I ask myself:
Is this an act of logic,
thought, of mind and body
consonant in grace?

And wonder still.

The hand of little occupation,
says Hamlet,
has the daintier sense.
So I, never a swimmer
in my youth, may have
a sense for this: piercing
the thick skin of the surface
like a porpoise, cresting
into my unbroken lane
with the ease of a schooner,
ratcheting my newly muscled arms
like turnstiles as I cruise,
tight-lipped and under my own power
among the icebergs and
coral and imaginary fishes.

And so this small oblation
to some unknown god,
this winsome ritual
in which body and mind
conspire to relieve themselves,
continues. And, in its wake,
all infidelities of kin and kind,
all indiscretions, wash away
and are forgiven. And I,
who once thought I was oil,
who once wanted to burn
beyond my own brief tenure,
am now content merely to be
that small vision of art
I am: a watercolor fading
in the hydrous light, a flame
that flickers and burns on,
a wick that brightens as it burns,
a small orbit of light, continuing.

In some species of fish,
the bluehead wrasse, for example,
or the Mexican hogfish,
there is a sea change, a transformation
that takes place in water, slowly,
at first subtle, but then
flamboyant, far-reaching, gaudy
and polychromatic. Sweeping now
through the water, sure
of my own manhood, but amenable
to possibilities, I wonder
what small protandry, what
hermaphroditic hope, lies dormant
within me, what womanish ambitions
my body dreams of as it rides
the lanes of its own moving,
as some sweet, hormonal urge
surfaces to suggest itself
and then diminishes. But
I would not have been lovely
as a woman, I know it,
I would not have surfaced
all dappled and luminous and
wildly desirable from such
a changing, as the groupers do
or the indigo hamlet, but simply
homely, confused, uncertain
of my own sensuousness.

So I see it is best
merely to continue
in the small confines
of my own being, to hear
the hard, turgid ripplings
of my pectorals
beneath the water, to watch

the curled adumbrations of
my body against the concrete,
to dream of another life,
womanish perhaps
and tenderer than this one,
and move on: all manly and
constant and lovely
in the water, transformed
only by this music, the sound
of my own body, singing.

Why get married,
my friend Bob
once said, *if*
you can't take a joke?
And so I think, turning now
for the twenty-sixth time,
why swim if you don't
see the humor in it,
the sheer whimsy
of beginning with no purpose
larger than boredom
and the body, then moving on
from there to something
larger, almost stupendous
in its implications?

And if life, friends,
is boring, why not say so,
why not simply chuckle
into your sleeve like a snail
and inch forward, at
whatever pace your arms
will carry you? Why not
stroke past the cold stone
of the self, lifting it
from its own density, moving it
quietly along the surface
until it rises like smoke,
like a gull's shadow,
over the tideless calm,
until you feel, as
the saying goes, *in*
the swim of things again?

I have heard certain women say
that, while pregnant,
they could sometimes hear
the sound of their own child
weeping, tears running down
its still unformed cheeks
into the womb, sobs
issuing forth into the night.

Now,
a sudden sadness
comes over me
as I sweep to turn,
and I wonder what it would be like
to cry into my own water,
to empty the warm ducts out
from my own eyes, adding
my wetness to the wet,
sending my sadness
through the swill
like the sound of stones
clicking under water.

Would anybody
notice? Would the pool
overflow, shedding
my hot brine over the sides
like an aborted fetus? Or would
I be merely a man crying *mother*
too late into his own life?
Would I be merely a swimmer
looking for comfort in the
wrong cavity, someone who
ought to control himself, bite
down hard on his manly lips,
and just swim on?

Repentance and forgiveness,
Steinsaltz says,
are the Jew's sacraments,
so here in these baptismal waters
I am one stroke forgiveness,
one repentance (these gestures
cover all I know), my arms
arcing like the back of a sunflower
over the surface as I realize,
again, why I am doing this:
because swimming is a kind
of forgetting, and there are days,
like today, when I would like
to forget all I have done, all
that has been done to me,
and merely swim.

And so I ask myself, while turning:
Is grief sincere? Or is
a merely wetness in the face
enough to move a man from grief
to joy? A fervent yahoo
in the balls now overtakes
my sense: the tragic washes off
to whence it came, and I'm
alive again, a bathing-suited lump
of pectorals and lust,
a man so eager to be cleansed
of all *tristesse*
he stoops to stroke
this wet, amorphous circumstance,
this sometimes antimetaphysical and
    happy plunge.

Wakes you up,
I will mumble
to the woman
in the elevator
as we head back
toward the locker room,
sure wakes you up.

I say this
almost every night
to whomever
I am riding with, not
because it interests me,
but because it's
one of those banal
but relatively harmless
things, like *hello*,
one can say
to break the silence,
and there are so few things
one can think of
to say in an elevator.

Wakes you up,
I will say,
and she: *Sure does*.

If nothing mundane is divine,
as a poet once said,
then why, approaching,
the end of my ordinary ritual,
do I feel as if the seas
had parted, as if
I had been walking, all along,
on air, like some
long-legged and luminous
aquatic bird, aloft
over a shallow pond?

Or is the epiphanous,
perhaps, to be found
in the numinous ordinary:
the drooped stem
of some fiduciary flower,
the quotidian flickerings
of the moon,
the carnal tides?

In the water now,
I can see again
the gray-blue pupils
of my wife's eyes,
how in them at times
a decent wetness surfaces,
the primal call
of some antique emotion
aroused by nothing.

So I too now
am aroused by nothing
I have yet a name for—
rhapsodically elegant,
pouched and anonymous

among these hyperventilating
bodies, thinking out loud
to myself: *Just two more,
friends, and then home
to my mundane heaven.*

A deeply moral sense
now rises
as I flip to turn: a hint
that what I've paddled toward,
disguised as exercise,
is truth, an ardor
for what buried thought,
in motion, can reveal,
an urge to wash away,
by movement, what
these surfaces conceal.

I see now,
once again, how things
outgrow what moved them
to begin: the wintry ice
begun as snow, the tree
that learned to know
the ground as seed. What
was I thinking when at first
I undertook this natatory trek?
What nagging avarice
compelled me downward
through the wet? Who would
have thought, a mere
half mile ago, that I'd
end here: forgetting
why I came at all,
remembering
what I had so long struggled
to forget.

My mother
on her rented deathbed,
glassy-eyed and thin
as a swimmer, looked up
at me the day before she died.
It was 1959.
I was ten, afraid
of swimming, a child
so unsure of his own buoyancy
he saw all water
as some mean Charybdis,
a quicksand
one might fall in
and only drown
by struggling against.

But now, a man
of thirty-two
and crossing this pool
a last time
to honor my own age,
I rise
by my own power
and remember her:
how she faded into
the deep, quiet pool
of her own evening, how,
like a swimmer setting out
to swim to a place she will
not be returning from,
she fluttered her eyelids
beneath the blue waters
of her own dying, she circled
into the still air above the bed,
graceful as a dolphin,
turning back

into her own body
as I, swimming, turn now
for the last time,
allowing myself to look again
into the deep, fathomless blue
of her eyes, to look again,
as a man, at my own life,
its deep losses and found loves,
its sometimes frozen circumstances,
now thawing as I
move through them, surfacing
in order to begin again,
lifting myself out of the water
in order to enter my life
for the second time,
in order to enter it again
as a man, spirit and flesh,
swimming homeward at last
to my life, and to you,
who are reading this
in a pool of my own choosing.

Epilogue

Does the heart harbor the body
or the body heart? Are we
a thinking juice, entombed
against our flesh? Walking
homeward from the pool, my body
muscle-toned, my mind refreshed,
I'm the continuing of thoughts
like these in dehydrated air.

I see the lights of cars,
once prismed by the morning rain,
now clear. I smell the cheeses
aging and the stale croissants.
I hear the birds. I touch my bones,
now vertical, that swallow streets
and wonder if God really spoke
to Abraham, or Joseph dreamt of wheat.

I am the long cantata
of these thoughts. I am
the swimmer who now walks,
in open air, among the trees.
I am the orphaned son,
the blade, the resurrected lamb.
I am a man, conspiratorial
of mind and flesh, who passes
through these lanes, who thinks:
I swim, therefore I am.

THE
JUNIPER
PRIZE

This volume is the tenth recipient
of the Juniper Prize
presented annually by the
University of Massachusetts Press
for a volume of original poetry.
The prize is named in honor of Robert Francis,
who has lived for many years at
Fort Juniper, Amherst, Massachusetts.